WITHDRAWN

W9-BEX-338

Garden *Whimsy*

A P P L I Q U É

Dodgeville Public Library
139 S. Iowa St.
Dodgeville, WI 53533

American Quilter's Society
P. O. Box 3290 • Paducah, KY 42002-3290
www.AmericanQuilter.com

Garden *Whimsy*
APPLIQUÉ

Mickey Depre

Located in Paducah, Kentucky, the American Quilter's Society (AQS) is dedicated to promoting the accomplishments of today's quilters. Through its publications and events, AQS strives to honor today's quiltmakers and their work and to inspire future creativity and innovation in quiltmaking.

Editor: Shelley Hawkins
Copy Editor: Chrystal Abhalter
Graphic Design: Amy Chase
Cover Design: Michael Buckingham
Quilt Photos: Charles R. Lynch (unless otherwise noted)

Library of Congress Cataloging-in-Publication Data

Depre, Mickey.
  Garden whimsy appliqué / by Mickey Depre.
     p. cm.
   Summary: "Appliqué birds, cornstalks, flowers, ants and more with these designs. Pieced backgrounds enhance appliqué images. Detailed instructions for each project."-- Provided by publisher.
  ISBN 1-57432-906-5
  1. Machine appliqué. 2. Machine quilting. I. Title.

TT779.D475 2006
746.44'5041--dc22

                    2006003164

Additional copies of this book may be ordered from the American Quilter's Society, PO Box 3290, Paducah, KY 42002-3290, or call 1-800-626-5420 or online at www.AmericanQuilter.com.

Proudly printed and bound in the
United States of America

DEDICATION

To my soul mate, my husband, Paul – without your support both mentally and physically, I wouldn't be the person I am today. Thank you.

To my greatest creations, my children, Paul Jr. and Emily – thank you for keeping me on my toes as I race along the path of life with both of you. I anticipate the years to come as you both soar to great heights. I look forward to your shade.

ACKNOWLEDGMENTS

I would like to thank my parents and sisters for their support and encouragement, even when I'm sure they were shaking their heads in bewilderment. I have not always traveled the easy road, but they have helped carry the luggage.

To my friends, near and far, thank you for being a part of my journey. You have all had a hand in helping me reach this goal, and I am forever grateful.

To all my students, who have been great sources of knowledge and fulfillment, thank you for giving me a chance to share my love of fiber.

My gratitude goes to Bernina® of America, Inc., and the education staff of this wonderful company. Your enthusiasm for sewing is so contagious that I catch it again year after year. Thank you for sharing.

To Shelley Hawkins, Barbara Smith, Bonnie Browning, Amy Chase, and many other members of the AQS staff, thank you for enduring my perpetual questions and phone calls. You have made my learning experience a smooth education. It will always be my good fortune to have crossed your paths.

INTRODUCTION

Sewing and fiber have held a place in my life for as long as I can remember. My mother is quite the seamstress, having sewn for my sisters and me throughout our childhood. Many nights, I fell asleep to the sound of a sewing machine humming in the next room.

Even before learning to sew on a machine, I had been fascinated by all things fiber. Having been blessed with grandmothers and great aunts who shared their needle art specialties with me, I was enjoying embroidery, crochet, and hand sewing by the age of six. I also enjoyed drawing, thanks to my dad.

My husband's birthday gift to me in our first year of marriage was a quilting frame. Although we lived in an urban area, I had no knowledge of quilt shops, guilds, or community workshops. I basically learned to quilt on my own and with the aid of library books.

At this time, I was piecing all my quilts and cutting templates with scissors because the rotary cutter and mat were not known to me. My husband helped cut template pieces in the evening, providing me with a wonderful scapegoat when seams didn't match up.

As my experience evolved, one of my quilting buddies gave me a lesson in needle-turn appliqué. I tackled several hand-appliqué quilts in the next few years and had to learn to machine quilt to keep up with the flow of quilts and ideas that were rapidly overtaking my sewing area.

The final step was machine appliqué. My trial-and-error method of self-education was put to use. Along the way, I broke a few appliqué rules and discovered my own method. Through the use of a craft iron-on backing, I have eliminated traditional steps of turning edges, as well as the need for additional tear-away stabilizers. Instructions for this method are provided on pages 10–13.

My gardens are obviously a point of inspiration for my work. While I enjoy the gardens, I can honestly say the weeding part is not high on my list of fun activities. But when I am out in them, I always see a new creature or bloom that sets off my creative muse.

Prepare to meet some of the creatures that live with me in my gardens. I hope they bring a smile and a giggle or two to your home.

Enjoy the day,

Mickey Depre

Emily Depre

Photos by the author and Paul A. Depre Sr.

CONTENTS

APPLIQUÉ MY WAY

Quilt project instructions are for raw-edge appliqué. I use the iron-on backing Pellon® Décor-Bond® for this method (see Resource Guide, page 78). However, the patterns can be adapted to any traditional turned-edge hand or machine appliqué method by simply adding the appropriate turn-under allowance to each pattern piece.

Pellon Décor-Bond shapes, supports, stabilizes, and adds crispness to upholstery fabric for home decorating. These qualities make it ideal for use in appliqué wall quilts. It allows you to create images without having to turn edges for machine appliqué.

Important: To give the quilt a consistent texture and eliminate warping, I apply this backing to all the fabric in the quilt, including the appliqué pieces, background, and borders. It is applied to units that make up the backgrounds, and in some cases, before cutting pieces.

To use Décor-Bond for the quilts in this book, the following list provides necessary yardage amounts:

Décor-Bond Requirements

Project	Yards
BALANCED	3
FANCY "PANSEYS"	⅔
SHOVELED	2
TWINS	2
NESTED	1
CORNSTALK CANOPY	1½
HOT TOMATOES	½
LUNCH DATE	½
HUGS	1½
BUDS	2¼
RAINMAKERS	1½
DRAGONFLY DANCE	1¼

Décor-Bond Benefits

Natural interfacing qualities – Light-colored fabrics can be placed over dark fabrics without shadowing.

Soft and supple quilts – Quilts retain the ability to be folded, making it usable in traditional bed or lap quilts.

Ease of movement – Appliqué pieces retain the ability to be moved with ease while you audition them on the quilt top.

Holds its shape – Appliqué pieces are stabilized, so there's no fear of warping or frayed edges from handling.

Dimensional qualities – The use of several layers can achieve a trapunto-like effect.

Ability to freehand or trace – With the use of a light source, tracing an appliqué pattern onto the non-adhesive side of Décor-Bond is easy.

Quilts hang straight – Corners are square, edges are straight.

Eliminates stabilizer – There's no need for additional tear-away stabilizers in machine appliqué.

Reduces basting – It naturally grabs cotton batting, reducing wrinkles in the quilt top when quilting. Ironing both the backing fabric and quilt top to the batting results in a smooth and secure surface to quilt.

Fusing Instructions

1. Using a light source, such as a light box or sunny window, trace the wrong side of the appliqué pattern onto the felt-like side of the Décor-Bond. A #2 pencil is the best drawing tool because markers and pens can smear.

2. Cut out the traced pattern with a generous ¼" allowance around the edge.

3. With your iron on the cotton setting, follow the manufacturer's instructions to adhere the Décor-Bond to the selected fabric.

Ironing Tips

All ironing should be done with the fabric right side up on the glue side of the Décor-Bond. The iron never touches the Décor-Bond. The fabric should extend past it to protect your iron.

For larger appliqué pieces, start ironing in the middle and work out toward the edge to reduce wrinkles. If a wrinkle occurs, quickly lift the fabric from the Décor-Bond in that area and re-iron. Keep the iron moving over the surface to avoid shrinkage.

4. Once the Décor-Bond is adhered to the fabric, cut the image on the drawn line. For light-colored fabrics, cut just inside the drawn line to ensure your pencil markings do not show. The appliqué image now has a crisp, clean-cut edge.

Appliqué Instructions

1. Place an appliqué foot on your machine and use a new needle for the start of every project. Sewing through Décor-Bond tends to dull needles quickly. For thread, cotton or rayon creates wonderful appliqué edging. Use lingerie or bobbin thread in the bobbin to reduce bulk on the back of the appliqué.

2. Set your machine to satin stitch. The stitch width should generously cover the appliqué edge, approximately ⅜". You can keep the length of the stitch very short for a smooth satin edge, or lengthen the stitch for more open stitching.

A short stitch length was used on the flowers in BALANCED.

A longer stitch was used on the leaves in NESTED.

Stitch around the appliqué edge.

3. Arrange the appliqué pieces on the background. Stabilizer is not needed. The background and appliqué layers eliminate the need for additional stabilization. Begin stitching in the least-conspicuous area of the appliqué. Take one stitch and bring the bobbin thread to the front of the appliqué.

4. After stitching around the entire appliqué edge, use a hand needle to bring the three thread ends behind the background. Tie and knot these ends to prevent the stitches from coming undone, and trim.

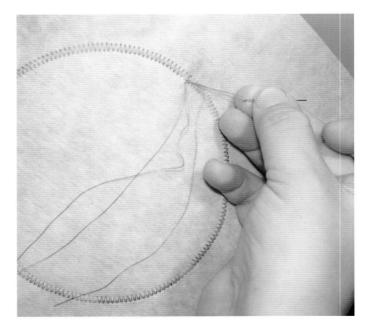

Bring the three thread ends behind the background.

5. The background and Décor-Bond should be removed from behind the appliqué to control the layers. With a seam ripper, gently poke a hole through the background and Décor-Bond layer and cut a hole approximately 1" in length. Use scissors to cut away the background and Décor-Bond, leaving a ¼" seam allowance from cut edge to sewn edge.

Machine quilting is the only method to finish any project with Décor-Bond due to its density. Quilting stitches are held to the front of your quilt, so all your hard work is shown off – no lost stitches tugged tightly into the batting. Stitches on the quilt back will also lie nicely because the natural tension tug from the top thread is minimal.

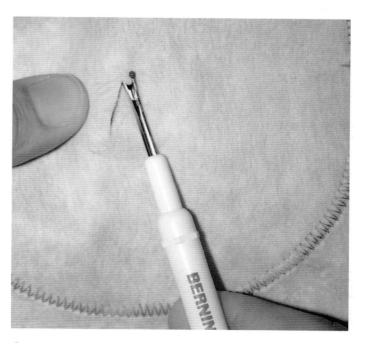

Cut a small hole in the Décor-Bond.

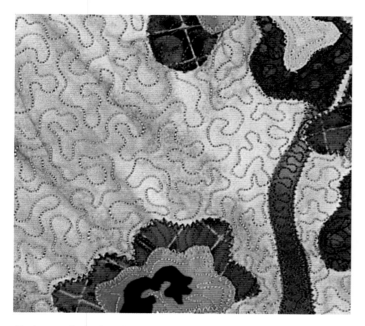

Background stipple quilting in *Fancy "Panseys."*

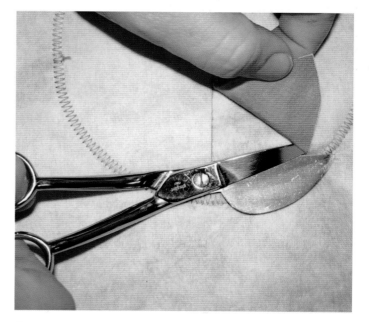

Cut away the background and Décor-Bond.

BALANCED

Size: 31" x 31"
Appliqué Technique:
Fusing Instructions, page 11
Appliqué Instructions, page 11

Many times, it is the spoken word rather than a visual image that inspires me. While writing this book, I worked some rather long hours in my studio. One day, my husband told me I needed to take a few days off in my life for balance. Later that evening, as I was relaxing with him and supposedly watching a movie, this quilt was being drawn in my mind. It took everything I had to wait for him to go to bed before I reached for my sketchbook.

Materials & Cutting

Material	Yards	Location	Cut
Blue	⅔	background	one 19½" square
			four 2½" x 19½" strips
Green	⅓	border	four 4½" x 19½" strips
Orange	⅙	Nine-Patches	two 2½" x 12" strips
			one 2½" x 21" strip
Black	⅙	Nine-Patches	one 2½" x 12" strip
			two 2½" x 21" strips
Appliqué	scraps		pattern, page 17
Batting			33" x 33"
Backing	1		33" x 33"
Binding	⅓		four 2½" x 42" strips

Border Assembly

1. Sew a 2½" blue strip to a 4½" green strip lengthwise. Press the seam allowances toward the green strip to complete a border unit. Repeat with the remaining three pairs of strips.

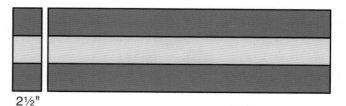

2½"

Strip-set 2 – cut into eight segments

2. To make the Nine-Patches, begin by sewing one black and two orange 12" strips together lengthwise as shown for strip-set 1. Press the seam allowances toward the black fabric. Trim 1" from the short edge of the strip-set to provide a straight edge for measuring. Cut the strip-set into four 2½" segments.

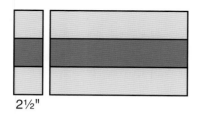

2½"

Strip-set 1 – cut into four segments

3. Repeat step 2 with one orange and two black 21" strips for strip-set 2. Cut the strip-set into eight 2½" segments.

4. Sew one segment from strip-set 1 and two segments from strip-set 2 together as shown to form a Nine-Patch. Iron the seam allowances toward the center. Make four Nine-Patches.

Nine-Patch assembly

5. Refer to the quilt assembly diagram on page 16 and sew the border unit from step 1 to the background square on two opposite sides. Press the seam allowances toward the borders. Sew a Nine-Patch to each end of the remaining border units. Make sure the Nine-Patch and border unit seams match. Press the seam allowances toward the border units. Sew this pieced border to the remaining sides of the quilt and press the seam allowances toward the quilt edge.

Appliqué

1. Photocopy the appliqué pattern on page 17 at 375%. After enlarging, the pattern lines appear thicker. Be sure to consistently use the outside edge of the pattern lines for cutting templates to ensure success.

2. Prepare the appliqué pieces for your chosen method of appliqué. If you are using iron-on backing, apply it to the appliqué fabrics.

3. Center the appliqué pattern on the background. Flowers should extend into the bottom border, and part of each bird will extend into the top and side borders. Follow numerical order to appliqué the pieces to the background. Each flower contains two parts – a center and a petal base. Join the two parts prior to stitching them to the background.

Finishing

Layer the quilt top, batting, and backing. Quilt the layers and bind your quilt. Don't be afraid to venture away from stippling your background. As long as thread color matches the fabric and the pattern is consistent, it will still recede. A loopy shell pattern stitched in the bird body gives the impression of feathers, while adding to the whimsy.

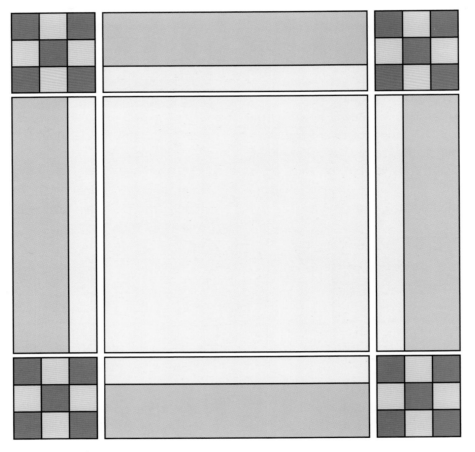

Fig. 4. Quilt assembly

Enlarge 375%

Appliqué a piece with an asterisk (*)
to the underlying piece, then appliqué
the unit to the background.

FANCY "PANSEYS"

Size: 18¼" x 16¾"
Appliqué Technique:
  Fusing Instructions, page 11
  Appliqué Instructions, page 11

Pansies greet me every spring in my garden. Their smiling faces cheer me up while I unpack all of the garden stuff. Their motivation works wonders as even the kids are inclined to wash off lawn furniture in anticipation of the gardens and late summer nights. *"Panseys" is the author's whimsical spelling.*

Materials & Cutting

Material	Yards	Location	Cut
Pink-green print	⅓	background	one 10¾" x 12¼" rectangle
Blue	⅓	binding	three 2½" x 42" strips
		side border	two 1½" x 12¼" strips
		top and bottom border	two 1½" x 18¼" strips
Blue-green print	¼	side border	two 3½" x 12¼" strips
		top and bottom border	two 1¾" x 18¼" strips
Appliqué	scraps		pattern, page 20
Batting			20¼" x 18¾"
Backing	⅝		20¼" x 18¾"

Appliqué

1. Photocopy the appliqué pattern on page 20 at 150%. After enlarging, the pattern lines appear thicker. Be sure to consistently use the outside edge of the pattern lines for cutting templates to ensure success.

2. Prepare the appliqué pieces for your chosen method of appliqué. If you are using iron-on backing, apply it to the appliqué fabrics.

3. Center the appliqué pattern on the background. Follow numerical order to appliqué the pieces to the background.

Quilt Assembly

Sew the inner side borders to each vertical edge of the appliqué background. Press the seam allowances toward the borders. Then, sew the outer side borders, the top and bottom inner borders, and the top and bottom outer borders to the quilt, pressing the seam allowances outward each time.

Quilt assembly

Finishing

Layer the quilt top, batting, and backing. Quilt the layers and bind your quilt. In simple appliqué designs, use multicolored prints in the border. Let the fabric work for you.

Enlarge 150%

Size: 20" x 32"
Appliqué Technique:
Appliqué Instructions, page 11
Fusing Instructions, page 11

The tools of the garden become good friends because they spend the winter cooped up in the storage shed. When the weather breaks, they all come out for the once-over – a blade sharpening and general hose down.

The short-handled shovel spends most of the spring dividing the perennials that need some breathing room and digging new homes for them. We sometimes forget to put the shovel away, so it takes up residence in the garden along with the "re-housed" plants.

Materials & Cutting

Material	Yards	Location	Cut
Light blue	¼	checkerboard	three 2½" x 9" strips
			four 2½" x 12" strips
Medium blue	¼	checkerboard	four 2½" x 9" strips
			three 2½" x 12" strips
Multicolor print	¾	bottom background	one 14½" x 15¼" rectangle
		side border	two 3¼" x 29¼" strips
		top border	one 3¼" x 20" strips
Dark blue	½	binding	three 2½" x 42" strips
		wavy border	one 6" x 34" strip
Appliqué	scraps		pattern, page 24
Batting			22" x 34"
Backing	¾		22" x 34"

Background and Borders

1. For Unit 1, sew seven 12" strips of light and medium blue together lengthwise in the order shown. Press the seam allowances toward the medium fabric. If necessary, trim the pieced unit to achieve straight edges. Cut Unit 1 into four 2½" segments.

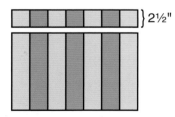

Unit 1 – cut four segments

2. For Unit 2, repeat step 1 with the 9" strips, alternating light and medium blue as shown. Cut Unit 2 into three 2½" segments.

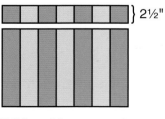

Unit 2 – cut three segments

3. Arrange Unit 1 and 2 segments in seven rows. Nestle the vertical seams of the squares and pin each seam intersection for precision. Sew the segments together for a 14½" square checkerboard background.

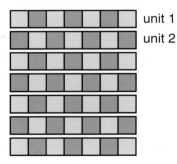

Checkerboard background assembly

4. Sew the bottom background piece to the checkerboard and press the seam allowances toward the rectangle.

5. Sew the side borders to the pieced background. Press the seam allowances toward the borders. Then, sew the top border to the quilt top and press the seam allowances toward the top border.

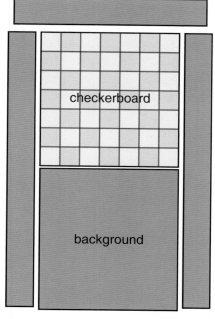

Quilt top assembly

Appliqué

1. If you are using iron-on backing, apply it to the wavy border strip. Refer to Cutting Wavy Borders (right) to cut three borders from the dark blue strip. You will use only 20" of the third border cut for the top of the quilt.

2. Lay a wavy strip on each side border, covering the long seams between the background and border. The strips will extend past the edges of the quilt. Appliqué the strips to the background, then cut away excess fabric behind the strips. Trim the strips even with the quilt.

3. Lay the third wavy strip along the seam between the background and top border, and repeat step 2 to appliqué.

4. Photocopy the appliqué pattern on page 24 at 400%. After enlarging, the pattern lines appear thicker. Be sure to consistently use the outside edge of the pattern lines for cutting templates to ensure success.

5. Prepare the appliqué pieces for your chosen method of appliqué. If you are using iron-on backing, apply it to the appliqué fabrics.

Cutting Wavy Borders

Place the strip on a cutting mat with the backing side up. Use a rotary cutter (45mm size preferably) to cut a soft, wavy line along the length of the strip. The difference between the hills and valleys of the wave should be approximately 1" and they should be nonsymmetrical to add visual appeal to your design.

Drawing the wavy lines in pencil is helpful if you are nervous about making a freehand cut. Another method for creating the wavy lines is to cut a sheet of freezer paper the size of your fabric strip. You can either draw a wavy line on the freezer paper with a pencil, or if confident enough, cut it with a rotary cutter.

Cut additional waves starting approximately 1" from the first cut. The cut should be opposite from the first at several intervals to create visual interest. Strip width should be between 1" and 1½" throughout the length. Strips with areas narrower than ½" will be hard to appliqué.

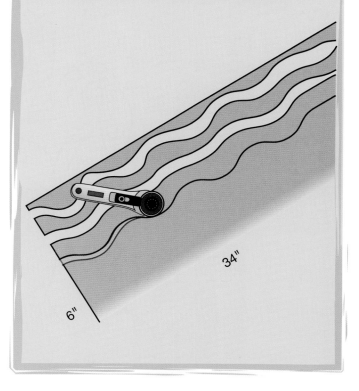

6. Center the appliqué pattern on the background so that the bottom edge of the grass aligns with the quilt edge so it will be caught in the binding.

7. Follow numerical order to appliqué the pieces to the background. Flower petals contain two parts. Join the two layers prior to stitching them to the background.

Finishing

Layer the quilt top, batting, and backing. Quilt the layers and bind your quilt. Take time to give the background sections, such as the checkerboard, wavy lines, and borders, individual quilting patterns.

Enlarge 400%

Appliqué a piece with an asterisk (*) to the underlying piece, then appliqué the unit to the background.

I am the lucky mother of twins – a son and daughter. I call them my buy-one-get-one-free special, although the free part doesn't apply. My husband and I count our blessings daily as we share these magical teenage years with Paul Jr. and Emily. Then we count the years to college, when we have told them we will rent the apartment for the first college that accepts them both.

My husband adopted a saying when the kids were born. When asked how hard it was raising twins, he would reply, "I don't know how hard it is because we have never had just one." I think this way of looking at things best describes our family attitude.

Materials & Cutting

Material	Yards	Location	Cut
Peach	fat quarter	background	one 17½" x 22" rectangle
Orange	¼	inner side border	two 1" x 22" strips
		inner top and bottom border	two 1" x 18½" strips
Blue-green	½	border squares	two 2½" x 42" strips
		outer border	four 4½" x 10½" rectangle
Purple	¼	border squares	two 2½" x 42" strips
Appliqué	scraps		pattern, page 28
Batting			28½" x 33"
Backing	⅞		28½" x 33"
Binding	⅓		four 2½" x 42" strips

Appliqué

1. Photocopy the appliqué pattern on page 28 at 300%. After enlarging, the pattern lines appear thicker. Be sure to consistently use the outside edge of the pattern lines for cutting templates to ensure success.

2. Prepare the appliqué pieces for your chosen method of appliqué. If you are using iron-on backing, apply it to the appliqué fabrics.

For the flower centers, cut two yellow oval background pieces. Then, cut two orange A stripes for each flower and appliqué them to the ovals. Cut two orange B stripes and appliqué them over the A stripes as shown.

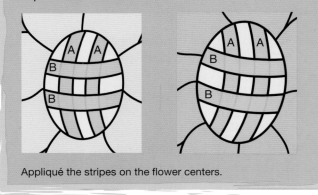

Appliqué the stripes on the flower centers.

3. Center the appliqué pattern on the background, aligning the grass edge with the bottom background edge so it will be caught in the seam allowance when piecing.

4. Follow numerical order to appliqué the pieces to the background. Appliqué the circles to the flower petals before they are appliquéd to the background. The stripes on the leaves can be created with an iron-on adhesive or they can be machine embroidered. Appliqué the stripes and inner part of the leaf before applying the leaf to the background.

Quilt Assembly

1. Sew each inner border strip to the sides of the appliqué background, then to the top and bottom. Press the seam allowances toward the borders.

2. For the outer border squares, sew the blue-green and purple 2½" strips together lengthwise. Iron the seam allowances toward the purple fabric. Repeat with the second strips. Cut the strips into twenty-eight 2½" wide segments.

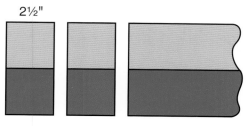

2½"

Border square strip-set – cut 28 segments

3. Sew the segments together, rotating them for a continuous checkerboard pattern, to form four Six-Patch units and four Eight-Patch units.

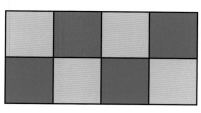

Eight-Patch Unit

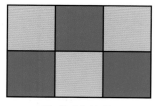

Six-Patch Unit

4. Arrange the outer border strips and the Six- and Eight-Patch units as shown in the quilt assembly diagram. Make sure the units are in the same position on all four corners.

5. Sew a Six-Patch unit to each short end of two border strips. Press the seam allowances toward the border strip. Sew this pieced border to each side of the quilt. Press the seam allowances toward the inner border.

6. Sew an Eight-Patch unit to each short end of the remaining border strips. Press the seam allowances toward the border strip. Sew this pieced border to the top and bottom of the quilt. Press the seam allowances toward the inner border.

Finishing

Layer the quilt top, batting, and backing. Quilt the layers and bind your quilt. Directional quilted lines in the flower petals add depth to solid-reading fabrics.

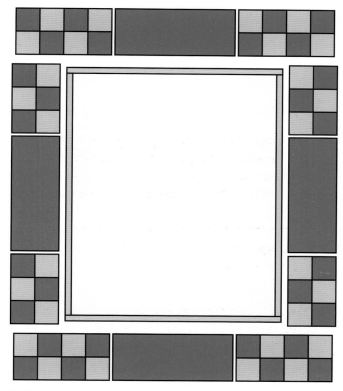

Quilt assembly

Enlarge 300%

Appliqué a piece with an asterisk (*)
to the underlying piece, then appliqué
the unit to the background.

NESTED

Three years ago, we lost our beloved ash tree in a rainstorm. This tree towered above our entire yard, plus a few of the neighbors' yards, and provided shade to all. It was also the home to a great deal of wildlife and a haven for many birds. We watched this neighborhood of nature through our window for many hours.

When the tree came down, it brought sunshine to areas of our yard that hadn't seen light for many years. The flowers rejoiced and grew to heights never seen before. Most of the wildlife found other places to reside on the block, including the new trees we planted.

Size: 23½" x 20"
Appliqué Technique:
Fusing Instructions, page 11
Appliqué Instructions, page 11

Materials & Cutting

Material	Yards	Location	Cut
Blue	⅜	background	one 16" x 12½" rectangle
Olive	⅓	border strip-set	two 2" x 3½" A rectangles
		border units	two 1½" x 16" C strips
			two 2½" x 16" D strips
			two 1½" x 12½" F strips
			two 2½" x 12½" G strips
		corner units	four 1¾" x 2¾" I rectangles
			four 1¾" x 4" J rectangles
Black	⅓	binding	three 2½" x 42" strips
		border strip-set	two 2" x 6¾" B rectangles
			two 2" x 5" E rectangles
		corner units	four 2¾" H squares
Appliqué	scraps		pattern, page 32
Batting			25" x 21½"
Backing	⅝		25" x 21½"

Appliqué

1. Photocopy the appliqué pattern on page 32 at 200%. After enlarging, the pattern lines appear thicker. Be sure to consistently use the outside edge of the pattern lines for cutting templates to ensure success.

2. Prepare the appliqué pieces for your chosen method of appliqué. If you are using iron-on backing, apply it to the appliqué fabrics.

3. Center the appliqué pattern on the background, aligning the tree trunk edge with the background edge so it will be caught in the seam when piecing. It is important that the tree trunk extends at least ½" past the background on the top, bottom, and side. After appliquéing, trim the tree even with the background seam allowance.

4. Follow numerical order to appliqué the pieces to the background.

Note that pieces 1, 19, 20, 21, 22, 24, and 25 fall behind other pieces, so the numbers appear in more than one location.

The leaf veins can be drawn with a fine-line, permanent ink pen or embroidered after the leaves have been appliquéd.

Quilt Assembly

1. To make the top and bottom border strip-set, sew a B rectangle to each side of an A rectangle. Cut the strip-set in half lengthwise for two strips that measure 1" x 16" each.

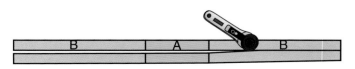

Border strip-set assembly

2. To make the side border strip-set, repeat step 1 with two E rectangles and the remaining A rectangle. The cut strips should measure 1" x 12½" each.

3. To make a border unit, sew a C strip to one side of the top strip-set. Then, sew a D strip to the other side. Repeat this process with the bottom border.

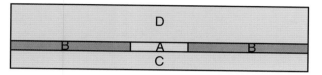

Top and bottom border unit assembly

4. Repeat step 3 to sew the F and G strips to the side strip-sets.

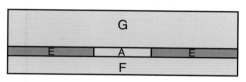

Side border unit assembly

5. To make a corner unit, sew an H square to an I rectangle. Then, sew a J rectangle across the top edge of two units and across the bottom edge of the remaining two units as shown. This keeps the seams aligned for a neat finished look to the quilt.

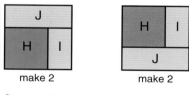

Corner unit assembly

6. Sew the top and bottom border units to the appliqué center as shown in the quilt assembly diagram. Iron the seam allowances toward the appliqué. Sew a corner unit to each end of the side border units, paying attention to the orientation of the corners. Press the seam allowances toward the corners. Sew the pieced borders to the side of the quilt top.

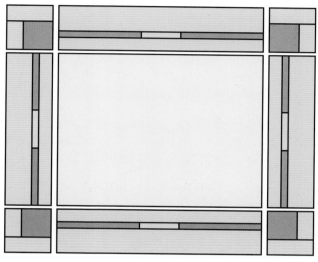

Quilt assembly

Finishing

Layer the quilt top, batting, and backing. Quilt the layers and bind your quilt. Texture can be achieved through an elongated swirl stitch on the tree trunk. Thread color that is slightly brighter or darker than the trunk fabric adds to this illusion.

Enlarge 200%

Size: 23" x 42¼"
Appliqué Technique:
Fusing Instructions, page 11
Appliqué Instructions, page 11

Lazy summer days are best spent in a hammock. Whether it is the shade of a tree or a couple of cornstalks, it's a great way to beat the midday heat. Grab a book and while away a few hours. Quite possibly, if you're like me, you will end up napping! Naps are good.

Materials & Cutting

Material	Yards	Location	Cut
Light blue	½	background	one 16½" x 28¾" rectangle
Appliqué	scraps		pattern, page 36
Dark blue	1¼	binding	five 2½" x 42" strips
		side border	two 3¾" x 28¾" strips
		top and bottom border	two 7¼" x 23" strips
Red	⅜	wavy border	one 12" x 42" strip
Batting			25" x 44¼"
Backing	1⅜		25" x 44¼"

Appliqué

1. Photocopy the appliqué pattern on page 36 at 300%. After enlarging, the pattern lines appear thicker. Be sure to consistently use the outside edge of the pattern lines for cutting templates to ensure success.

2. Prepare the appliqué pieces for your chosen method of appliqué. If you are using iron-on backing, apply it to the appliqué fabric. Use an iron-on adhesive for the ant's arms and legs.

3. Center the appliqué pattern on the background. Align the bottom edge of the stem with the quilt edge so it will be caught in the seam when piecing.

4. Follow numerical order to appliqué the pieces to the background. A fine-line permanent ink pen was used to add detail to the corncobs. The corn tassels and straw in the ant's mouth can be completed with machine embroidery or thin strips of fabric adhered with lightweight fusible. The hammock patch was detailed with embroidery floss.

Quilt Assembly

1. Sew the side borders to the appliqué background. Press the seam allowances toward the borders. Then, sew the top and bottom borders to the background in the same manner.

2. If you are using iron-on backing, apply it to the wavy border strip. Refer to Cutting Wavy Borders on page 23 to cut four strips lengthwise.

3. Lay a wavy strip on each side border and pin in place. The waves will reach from top to bottom of the quilt. Do not appliqué the waves at this time.

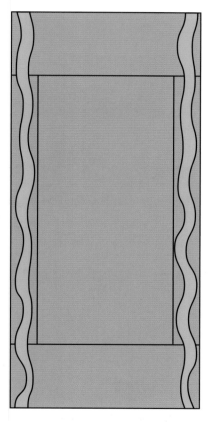

Pin a wavy strip on each side border.

4. Lay a wavy strip on the top and bottom borders, overlapping the side wavy strips. Play with the final placement of the strips. You will want a thicker area of the wave to overlap the side strips already in place. When satisfied, pin the top and bottom waves. Do not place pins within 5" of the intersecting waves

so you can flip back the top and bottom waves when appliquéing the side waves.

5. Trim each end of the side strips so they are covered by the top and bottom strips. Appliqué the side strips to the border fabric.

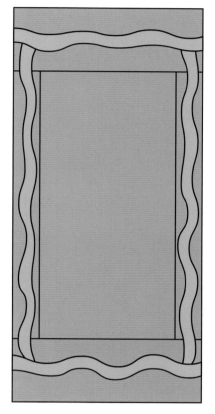

Trim the side strips so the top and bottom strips overlap them.

6. Trim each end of the top and bottom strips so that they create a continuous flow with the side strips. Appliqué the top and bottom strips to the border fabric.

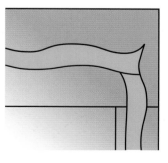

Trim the top and bottom strips, creating a continuous flow along the edge.

Finishing

Layer the quilt top, batting, and backing. Quilt the layers and bind your quilt. The gradation of the corn stalk quilting pattern from large to small draws the eye up to the corn ears.

Enlarge 300%

HOT TOMATOES

Size: 15" x 15"
Appliqué Technique:
Fusing Instructions, page 11
Appliqué Instructions, page 11

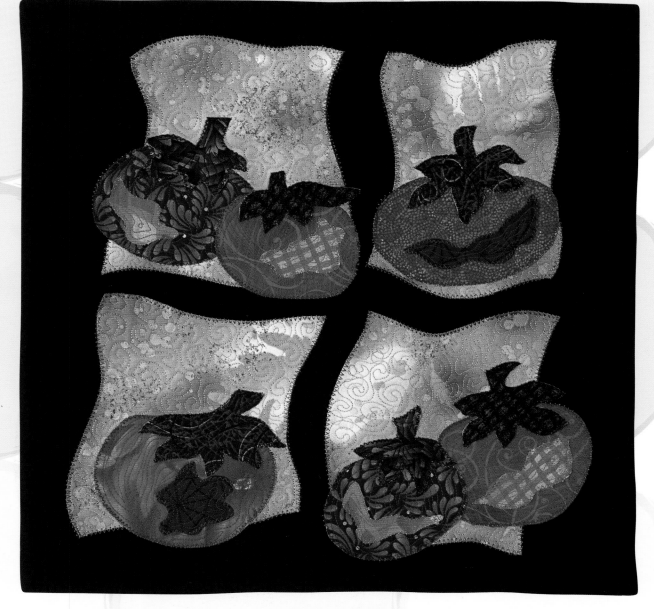

Paul Sr. is in charge of the vegetable garden. He plants it, tends to it, and of course, I help him devour it. Paul always plants many more veggies than the Depre family can possibly consume, so the neighbors, family, and even strangers walking down the street benefit from the bounty of our garden.

My favorites are all the varieties of tomatoes that the garden provides, from Beefmasters to Yellow Bells. Pass the blue cheese dressing and life is good.

Materials & Cutting

Material	Yards	Cut
Black	½	one 15" square
Appliqué	scraps	pattern, page 39
Batting		17" x 17"
Backing	½	17" x 17"
Binding	¼	two 2½" x 42" strips

Appliqué

1. Photocopy the appliqué pattern on page 39 at 200%. After enlarging, the pattern lines appear thicker. Be sure to consistently use the outside edge of the pattern lines for cutting templates to ensure success.

2. Prepare the appliqué pieces for your chosen method of appliqué. If you are using iron-on backing, apply it to the appliqué fabrics.

3. Center the appliqué pattern on the background, using the photo on page 37 as a reference. Follow numerical order to appliqué the pieces to the background.

Finishing

Layer the quilt top, batting, and backing. Quilt the layers and bind your quilt. The variety of fabrics from red/red to orange/red and prints, plus free-motion quilting with similar-colored thread, helps each tomato stand out.

Enlarge 200%

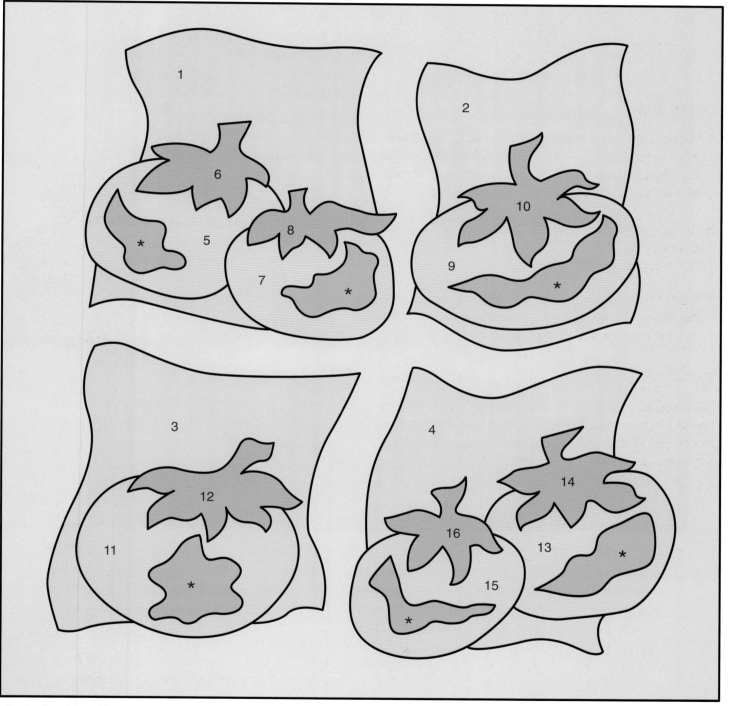

Appliqué a piece with an asterisk (*)
to the underlying piece, then appliqué
the unit to the background.

LUNCH DATE

Size: 15" x 15"
Appliqué Technique:
　Fusing Instructions, page 11
　Appliqué Instructions, page 11

My husband and I have been a couple for a great many years – we have prom pictures to prove it. We have faced many hills and valleys in our relationship, but have gotten through it all by keeping the communication lines open.

Paul Sr. works just a few blocks from home, so most everyday, we eat lunch together, whether he comes home or we meet at a restaurant. This child-free time is wonderful. We talk about our day so far and the evening to come, a project we're working on, or something happening in the world. But most importantly, we communicate.

Materials & Cutting

Material	Yards	Location	Cut
Light blue	⅜	background	one 9½" square
Green	⅛	inner side border	two 1½" x 9½" strips
		inner top and bottom border	two 1½" x 11½" strips
Blue	⅙	outer side border	two 2¼" x 11½" strips
		outer top and bottom border	two 2¼" x 15" strips
Appliqué	scraps		pattern, page 43
Batting			17" x 17"
Backing	⅝		17" x 17"
Binding	¼		two 2½" x 42" strips

Border Assembly

1. Sew the inner side borders to the appliqué background. Then, sew the inner top and bottom borders to the background. Press all seam allowances toward the borders.

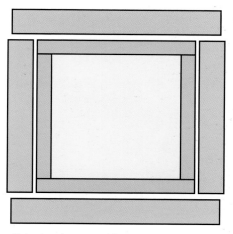

Outer border assembly

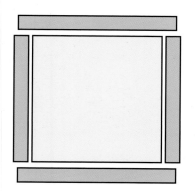

Inner border assembly

2. Sew the outer side borders to the quilt top. Then, add the outer top and bottom borders. Press all seam allowances toward the outer borders.

Appliqué

1. Photocopy the appliqué pattern on page 43 at 200%. After enlarging, the pattern lines appear thicker. Be sure to consistently use the outside edge of the pattern lines for cutting templates to ensure success.

2. Prepare the appliqué pieces for your chosen method of appliqué. If you are using iron-on backing, apply it to the appliqué fabrics.

3. Center the appliqué pattern on the background slightly below the center. The bottom flower petals should fall approximately 1" from the background edge. Position the appliqué image by using the quilt photograph as a reference.

4. Follow numerical order to appliqué the pieces to the background. Appliqué the hearts and black pieces to the bee bodies before they are appliquéd to the background. The small flower pieces and the bee sunglasses can be appliquéd after all other pieces have been appliquéd to the background. Use an iron-on adhesive for the bee antennae, or they can be drawn with a fine-line, permanent ink pen, but make the lines thick enough to be seen at a distance.

Finishing

Layer the quilt top, batting, and backing. Quilt the layers and bind your quilt. Quilting with metallic thread on the wing appliqué adds luminosity. A little goes a long way.

Enlarge 200%

Appliqué a piece with an asterisk (*)
to the underlying piece, then appliqué
the unit to the background.

Hugs

Size: 17½" x 29"
Appliqué Technique:
Fusing Instructions, page 11
Appliqué Instructions, page 11

On the first truly warm day of summer, I step outside and feel the warm embrace of the sun. I am like a child as I rejoice in the rays. If the neighbors couldn't see me over the fence, I would probably join the kids in running through the sprinkler.

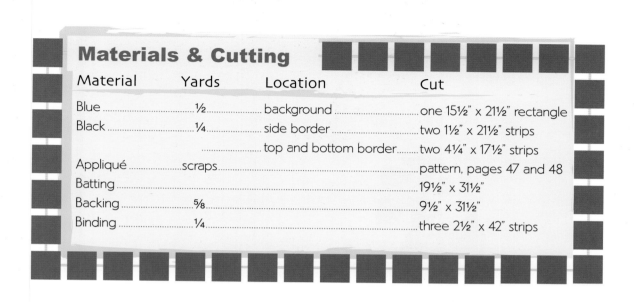

Materials & Cutting

Material	Yards	Location	Cut
Blue	½	background	one 15½" x 21½" rectangle
Black	¼	side border	two 1½" x 21½" strips
		top and bottom border	two 4¼" x 17½" strips
Appliqué	scraps		pattern, pages 47 and 48
Batting			19½" x 31½"
Backing	⅝		9½" x 31½"
Binding	¼		three 2½" x 42" strips

Appliqué

1. Photocopy the appliqué pattern on page 47 at 200%. After enlarging, the pattern lines appear thicker. Be sure to consistently use the outside edge of the pattern lines for cutting the templates to ensure success.

2. Prepare the appliqué pieces for your chosen method of appliqué.

For the sun center, cut the entire piece 13 from yellow fabric. Then, cut individual orange pieces to make the checkerboard pattern. If you are using iron-on backing, apply it to the appliqué fabrics.

3. Center the appliqué pattern on the background, aligning the bottom edge of the stem with the background edge so it will be caught in the seam when piecing.

4. Follow numerical order to appliqué the pieces to the background. The stripes and the dots should be appliquéd to the leaves and flowers, respectively, before they are appliquéd to the background.

5. Fold the top and bottom borders in half both lengthwise and widthwise to determine the center, and use the fold lines for positioning the center circle. Appliqué the circles to the top and bottom borders.

Quilt Assembly

Sew the side borders to the appliqué background. Press the seam allowances toward the borders. Sew the top and bottom borders to the quilt. Press the seam allowances toward the borders.

Finishing

Layer the quilt top, batting, and backing. Quilt the layers and bind your quilt. Note the directional fabric used in the border. Take time when cutting so the pattern reads upright on the sides, top, and bottom. This small detail adds to the visual appeal of your quilt.

Quilt assembly

Enlarge 200%

Appliqué a piece with an asterisk (*) to the underlying piece, then appliqué the unit to the background.

½ Border Appliqué
Full-size pattern

reverse pattern along line for other half

Sun Center
Full-size pattern

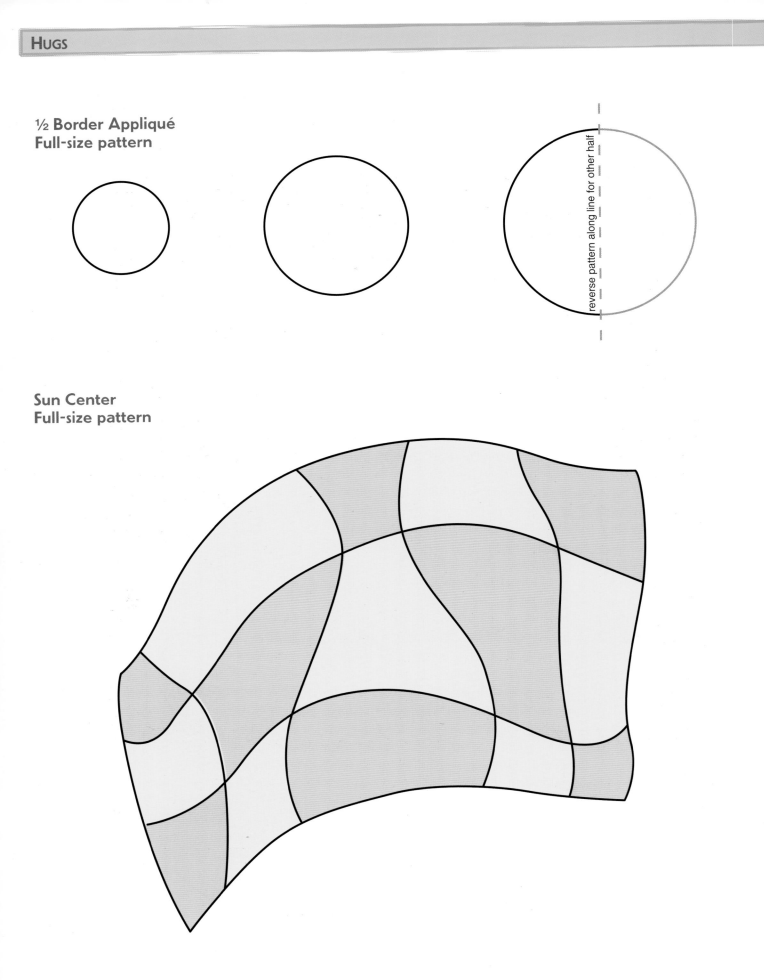

Size: 29" x 29"
Appliqué Technique:
Fusing Instructions, page 11
Appliqué Instructions, page 11

Friends are indeed the spice of life. They celebrate the good times and provide comfort in the not-so-good times. They allow you to grouse on the phone and still pick you up for the quilt guild meeting that night. Sometimes you go a few weeks without really talking, but pick right up when you are back in town.

Friends allow you to shop their fabric stash. They laugh with you while driving all over town visiting quilt shops, and they never ever rush you when you are trying to decide exactly which blue you need. In fact, they are so wise that they often suggest you purchase all three – one for the project and the other two for your stash. I am so grateful for my friends.

Materials & Cutting

Material	Yards	Location	Cut
Light blue	⅝	background	one 18½" square
Blue-green	1	binding	three 2½" x 42" strips
		border	four 2½" A squares
			eight 1½" x 2½" B rectangles
			twelve 2½" x 4½" C rectangles
			four 2½" x 14½" D strips
			two 2⅞" E squares
			two 1¾" x 18½" F strips
			eight 2½" x 3¾" G rectangles
			two 1¾" x 29" H strips
Yellow	¼	border	twenty-four 2½" A squares
			four 2½" x 4½" C rectangles
			two 2⅞" E squares
Red	⅛	border	eight 1½" x 2½" B rectangles
Appliqué	scraps		pattern, page 54
Batting			31" x 31"
Backing	1		31" x 31"

Appliqué

1. Photocopy the appliqué pattern on page 54 at 250%. After enlarging, the pattern lines appear thicker. Be sure to consistently use the outside edge of the pattern lines for cutting the templates to ensure success.

2. Prepare the appliqué pieces for your chosen method of appliqué. If you are using iron-on backing, apply it to the appliqué fabrics.

3. Center the appliqué pattern on the background, aligning the stems with the bottom background edge so they will be caught in the seam when piecing.

4. Follow numerical order to appliqué the pieces to the background. Use an iron-on adhesive for smaller elements of the design, such as the leaf details.

Border Assembly

Side borders

1. To make the center section of Unit 1, sew two red B rectangles, two blue-green B rectangles, and one blue-green A square together, as shown.

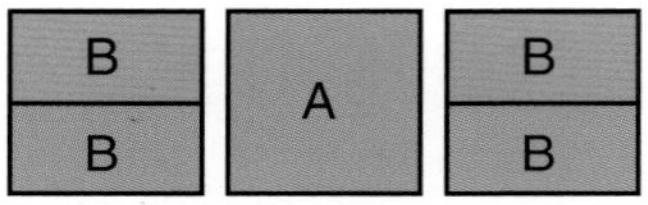

Unit 1 center section

2. Draw a diagonal line on the wrong side of two yellow A squares. Place the squares on opposite ends of two blue-green C rectangles, aligning the edges. Sew on the drawn lines. Trim the seam allowances to ¼" and press open.

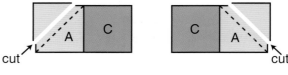

Unit 1 pieced rectangles

3. Sew a pieced rectangle to each end of the center section. Then, sew a yellow A square to each end of the strip to complete Unit 1.

Unit 1 assembly

4. To make the half-square triangles in Unit 2, place a blue-green and a yellow E square right sides together. Draw a diagonal line from corner to corner. Sew ¼" away from the line on each side. Cut on the drawn line and press the seam allowances toward the darker fabric.

Unit 2 half-square triangles

5. Sew a half-square triangle to each end of a blue-green D strip to complete Unit 2.

6. Sew Units 1, 2, and a blue-green F strip together as shown to complete one side border. Repeat steps 1 through 6 to make the second side border.

Top and bottom borders

1. Repeat steps 1 and 2 of the side border instructions to make a center section and pieced rectangles for Unit 3.

2. Sew a pieced rectangle to each end of the center section. Then, sew a yellow C rectangle to each end of the pieced strip, as shown in the last figure (Unit 3 section) below.

Unit 2 assembly

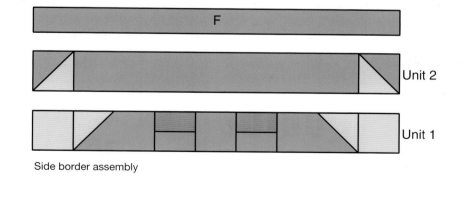

Side border assembly

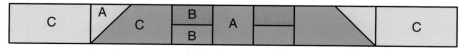

Unit 3 section

3. To make the last pieced rectangle for Unit 3, draw a diagonal line on the wrong side of two yellow A squares. Place the squares on opposite ends of two blue-green G rectangles. Sew on the drawn lines. Trim the seam allowances to ¼" and press open. Sew a pieced rectangle to each end of the Unit 3 section to complete Unit 3.

4. To make Unit 4, draw a diagonal line on the wrong side of two yellow A squares. Place an A square on the left side of a blue-green C rectangle, right sides together. Sew on the drawn line. Trim the seam

allowance to ¼" and press open. Repeat for the right side of the C rectangle. Make two of these pieced rectangles.

5. Sew a pieced rectangle to each end of a blue-green D rectangle. Sew a blue-green G rectangle to each end of the pieced strip to complete Unit 4.

6. Sew Units 3, 4, and the blue-green H strip together as shown in the top border assembly diagram to complete the top border. Repeat steps 1 through 6 to make the bottom border.

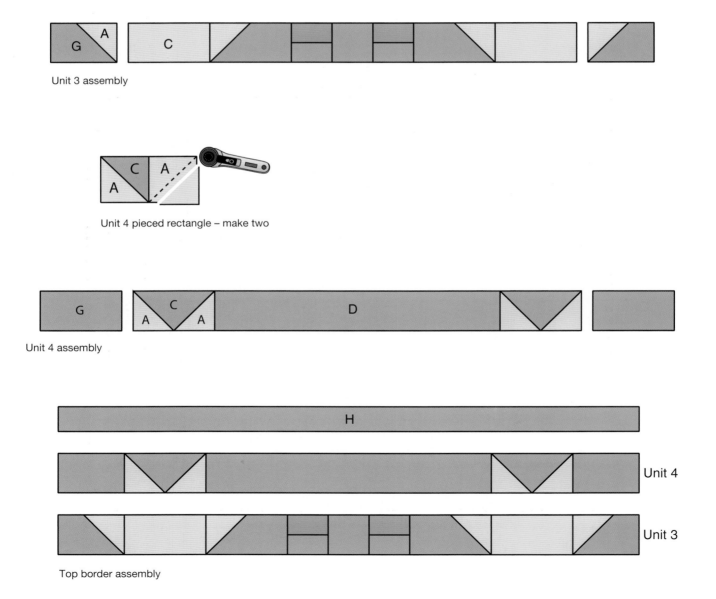

Unit 3 assembly

Unit 4 pieced rectangle – make two

Unit 4 assembly

Top border assembly

Quilt Assembly

1. Arrange the side borders, top and bottom borders, and center appliqué as shown in the quilt assembly diagram.

2. Sew each side border to the center appliqué. Then sew the top and bottom borders to the quilt top. Press all seam allowances toward the borders.

Finishing

Layer the quilt top, batting, and backing. Quilt the layers and bind your quilt. Tightly packed circles in the flower centers add great texture. The gradation of the flower stem quilting pattern from large to small draws the eye up to the flowers.

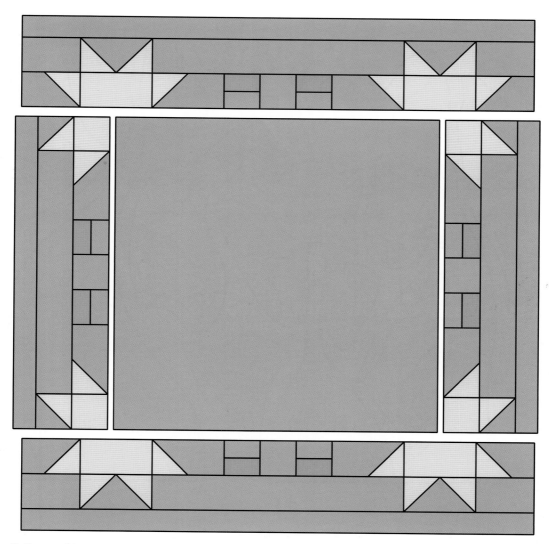

Quilt assembly

Enlarge 250%

Appliqué a piece with an asterisk (*) to the underlying piece, then appliqué the unit to the background.

RAINMAKERS

Watering our garden is quite the task because the backyard is almost entirely full of flowers – no grass, just flowers. Most of the time, Mother Nature takes care of the watering, but I make sure all my babies get a good drink once a week. If time permits, I like to water the entire garden by hand with my trusty watering can. This way, I can take a good look at each plant and say hello. Of course, Mother Nature confuses this exercise with a rain dance, and it usually rains within 24 hours of my watering.

Size: 29¾" x 20¼"
Appliqué Technique:
Fusing Instructions, page 11
Appliqué Instructions, page 11

Materials & Cutting

Material	Yards	Location	Cut
Peach	⅜	background	one 25¾" x 12" rectangle
Green	¼	background	one 25¾" x 4¾" strip
Blue	½	binding	three 2½" x 42" strips
		side border	two 2½" x 16¼" strips
		top and bottom border	two 2½" x 29¾" strips
Appliqué	scraps		pattern, page 57
Batting			31¾" x 22¼"
Backing	¾		31¾" x 22¼"

Appliqué

1. Photocopy the appliqué pattern on page 57 at 300%. After enlarging, the pattern lines appear thicker. Be sure to consistently use the outside edge of the pattern lines for cutting the templates to ensure success.

2. Prepare the appliqué pieces for your chosen method of appliqué. If you are using iron-on backing, apply it to the appliqué fabrics.

3. Center the appliqué pattern on the background using the photo on page 55 as a reference.

4. Follow numerical order to appliqué the pieces to the background. Appliqué the flowers from the center outward to ensure proper spacing. Cut the flower petals as one unit. The flower center will cover the fabric between the petals, which will appear to be individual pieces when complete.

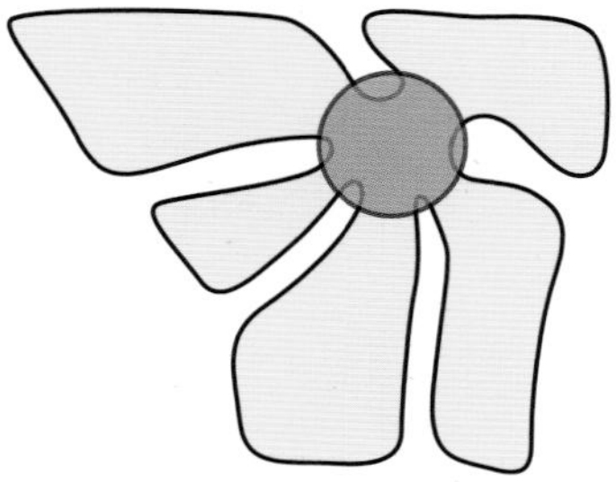

Flower petals are cut as a single piece.

Quilt Assembly

1. Sew the peach and green pieces together along the lengthwise edge. If you prefer, the designs can be appliquéd to the background prior to adding the borders. Just read ahead for the appliqué instructions.

2. Sew the side borders to the appliqué background. Then add the top and bottom borders. Press all seam allowances toward the borders.

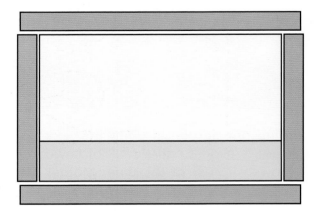

Quilt assembly

Finishing

Layer the quilt top, batting, and backing. Quilt the layers and bind your quilt. Densely packed flowers quilted in the background give the viewer a visual surprise.

Enlarge 300%

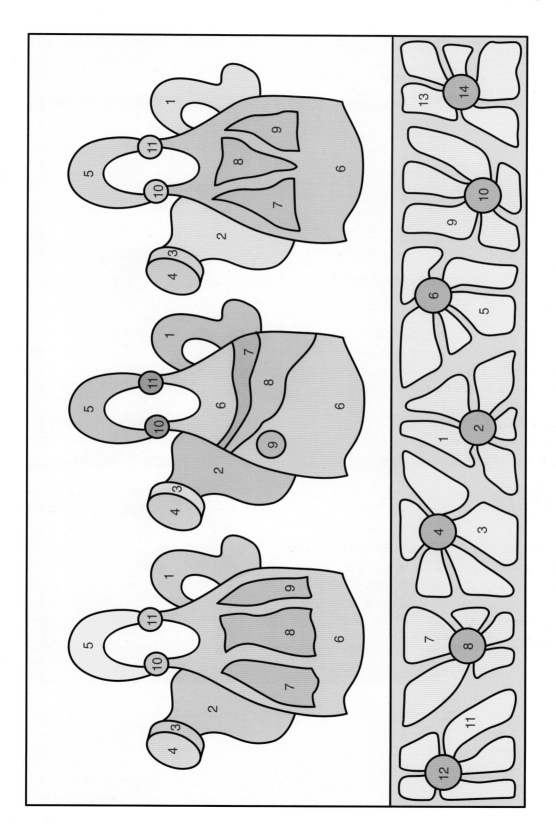

DRAGONFLY DANCE

Size: 22½" x 33½"
Appliqué Technique:
Fusing Instructions, page 11
Appliqué Instructions, page 11

My husband built a gazebo in the center of our yard. It is wired with electricity and cable so we can watch baseball games out there every evening. Many times, dragonflies join us for the opening pitch as they explore the gardens that encircle our outdoor "room." They have even landed on the tables next to our chairs. Their size and variety amaze me. Just when Paul has the camera on them, they dance away.

Materials & Cutting

Material	Yards	Location	Cut
Light blue	½	background	one 14½" x 25½" rectangle
Blue	¾	binding	four 2½" x 42" strips
		top and bottom border	two 4½" x 14½" strips
		side border	two 4½" x 33½" strips
Appliqué	scraps		pattern, page 61
Batting			24½" x 35½"
Backing	¾		24½" x 35½"

Appliqué

1. Photocopy the appliqué pattern on page 61 at 400%. After enlarging, the pattern lines appear thicker. Be sure to consistently use the outside edge of the pattern lines for cutting the templates to ensure success.

2. Prepare the appliqué pieces for your chosen method of appliqué. If you are using iron-on backing, apply it to the appliqué fabrics.

3. Center the appliqué pattern on the background, using the photo on page 58 as a reference.

4. Follow numerical order to appliqué the pieces to the background.

Appliqué the starred design to pieces 1–7 as separate units, then appliqué to the background.

The antennae and smaller elements of the design, such as the dots on the dragonfly body, may be embroidered or drawn.

Quilt Assembly

1. Sew the top and bottom border strips to each horizontal edge of the appliqué background. Press the seam allowances toward the borders.

2. Sew the side border strips to each vertical edge of the quilt top. Press the seam allowances toward the borders.

Border Appliqué

Tip
If you use a striped fabric for the wavy strips, cut the fabric so the stripes run widthwise for maximum impact. Lengthwise stripes will be "lost" in these ribbons.

1. Prepare the border appliqué pieces for your chosen method of appliqué. If you are using iron-on backing, refer to the manufacturer's directions for application.

2. Center the appliqué on the border, using the quilt photograph as a reference.

3. Follow numerical order to appliqué the pieces to the background. Cut the flower petals as one piece. The flower center will cover the fabric between the petals, which will appear to be individual pieces when complete.

Finishing

Layer the quilt top, batting, and backing. Quilt the layers and bind your quilt. A simple wavy grid quilted on the background gives a backdoor screen effect.

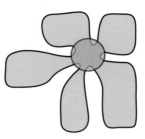

Flower petals are cut as a single piece.

Enlarge 400%

Appliqué a piece with an asterisk (*) to the underlying piece, then appliqué the unit to the background. Appliqué the small dragonflies in the same order as the larger one.

BONUS BLOCK PATTERNS

SIXTY-SIX DECO

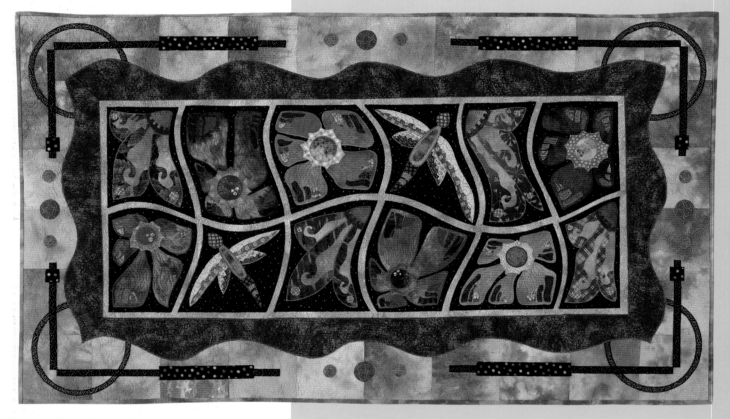

Size: 49" x 29"

SIXTY-SIX DECO was completed in the span of about two weeks. When I view this quilt, I see myself in every square inch. It is a true representation of my creative style in life, combining art deco elements with psychedelic 1960s' imagery for some fun!

While the author has set these charming motifs in irregular-shaped blocks, you can appliqué them to squares and rectangles instead, and you can mix and match them as desired for your own quilt projects. They can also be used for wearable and decorative items, such as clothing, pillows, and purses.

Quilt assembly

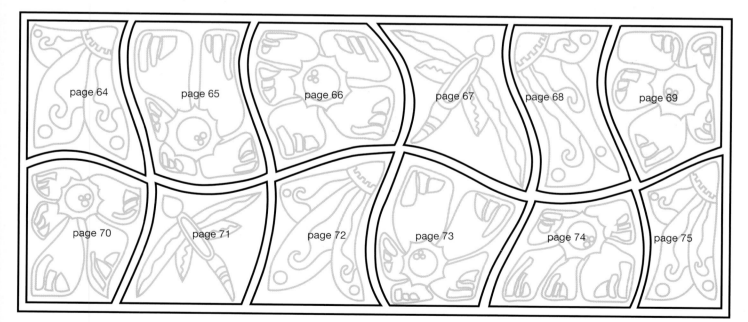

Pattern placement

Full-size pattern

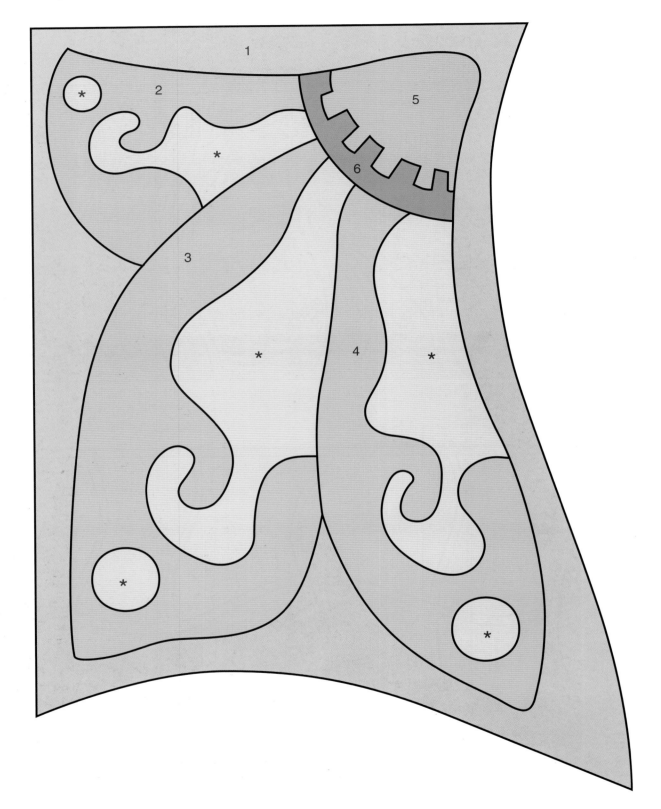

Appliqué a piece with an asterisk (*) to the underlying piece, then appliqué the unit to the background.

Full-size pattern

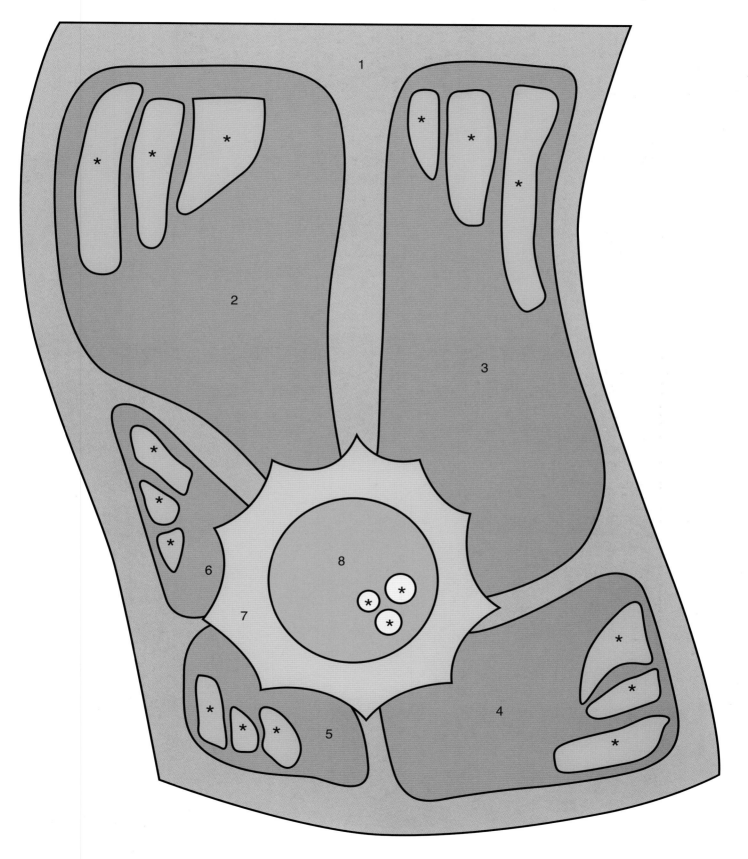

Full-size pattern

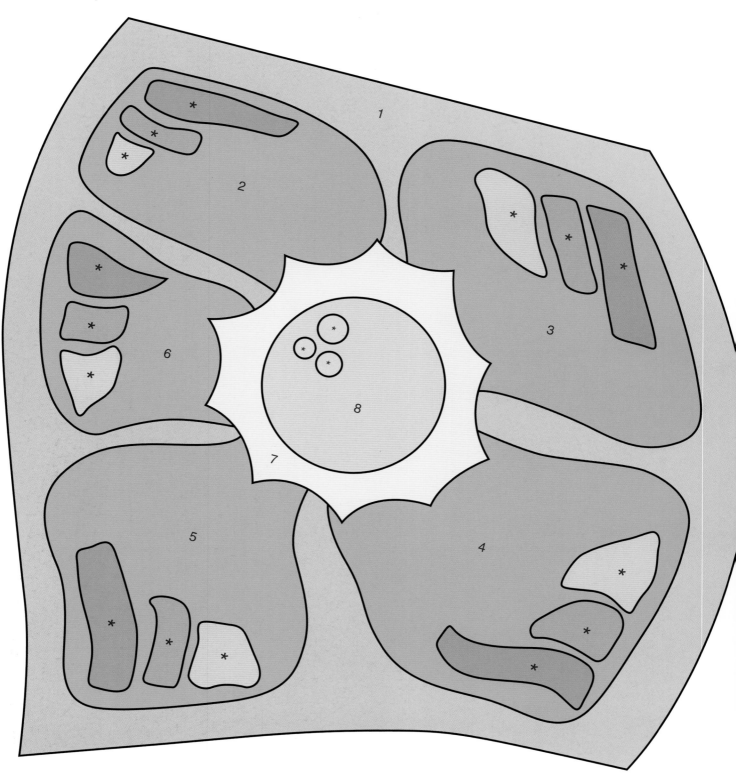

Appliqué a piece with an asterisk (*) to the underlying piece, then appliqué the unit to the background.

Full-size pattern

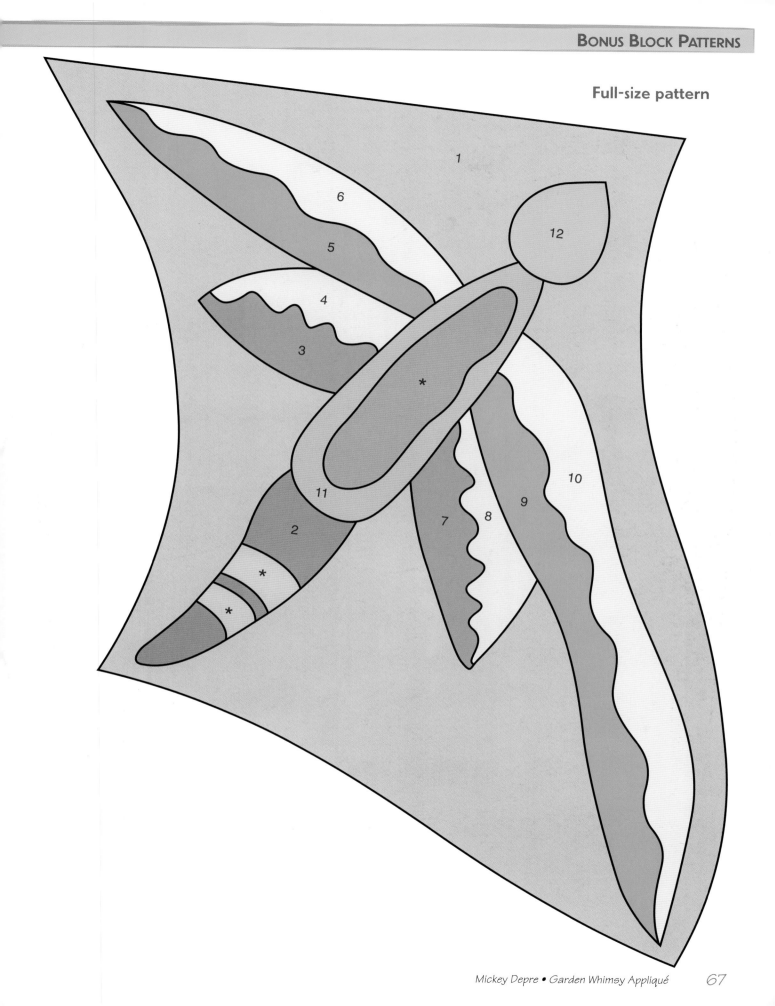

Full-size pattern

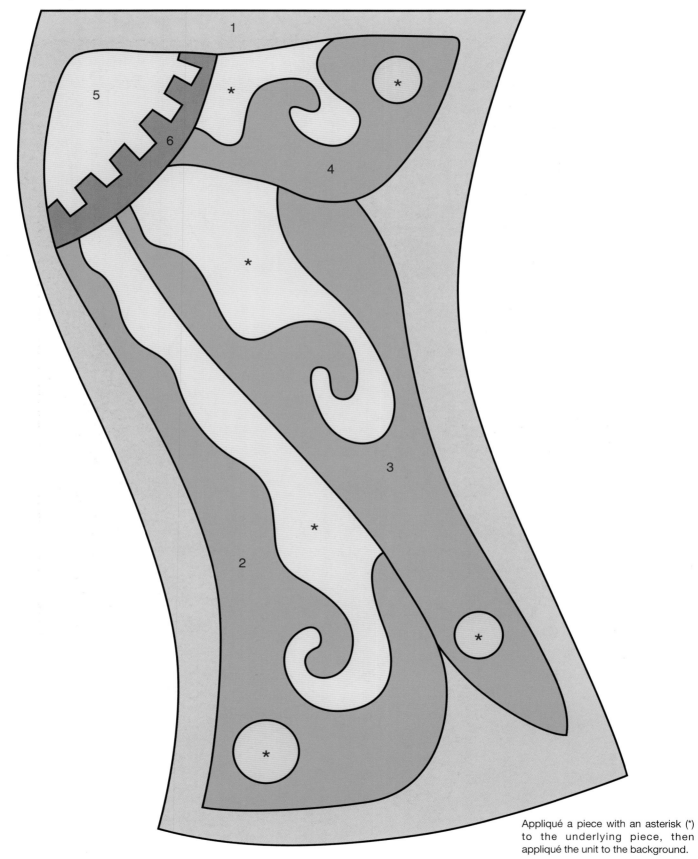

Appliqué a piece with an asterisk (*) to the underlying piece, then appliqué the unit to the background.

Full-size pattern

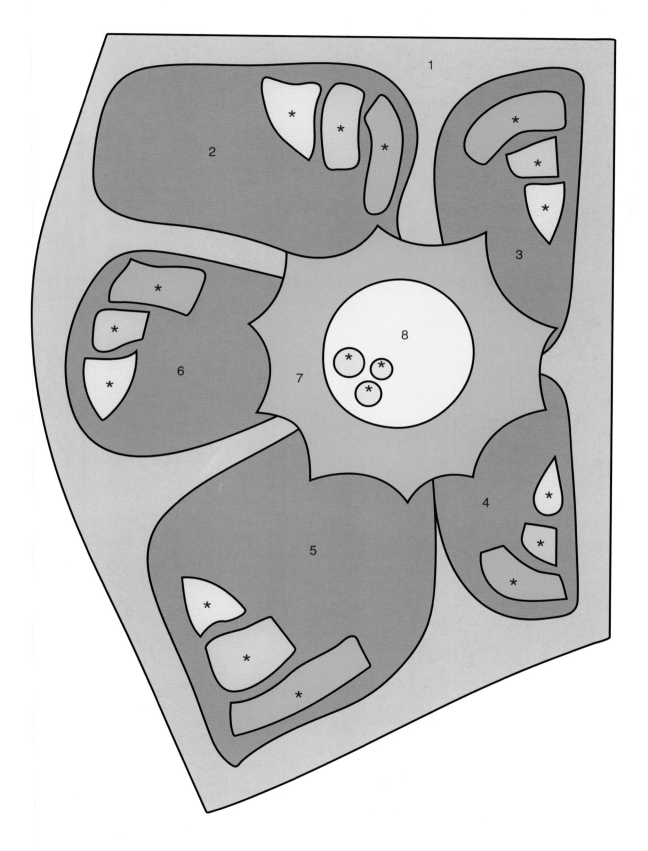

Full-size pattern

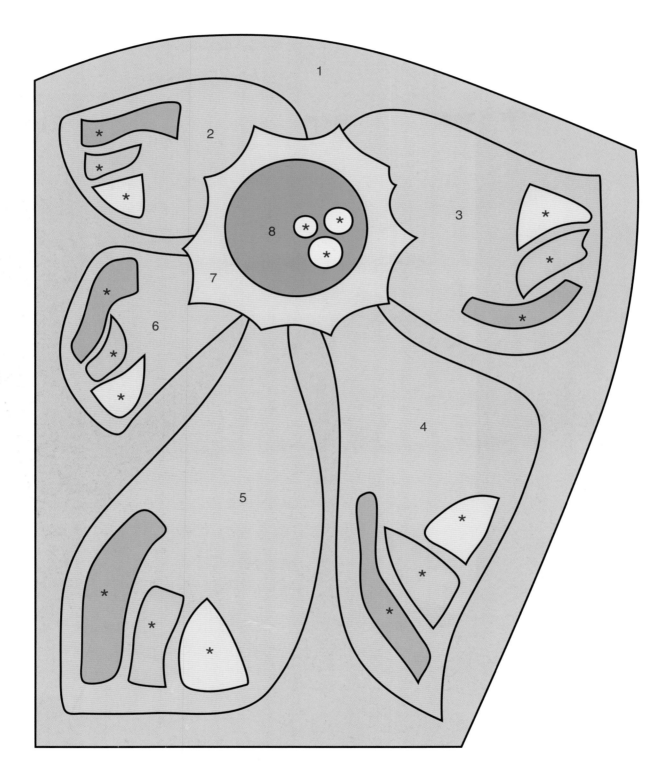

Appliqué a piece with an asterisk (*) to the underlying piece, then appliqué the unit to the background.

Full-size pattern

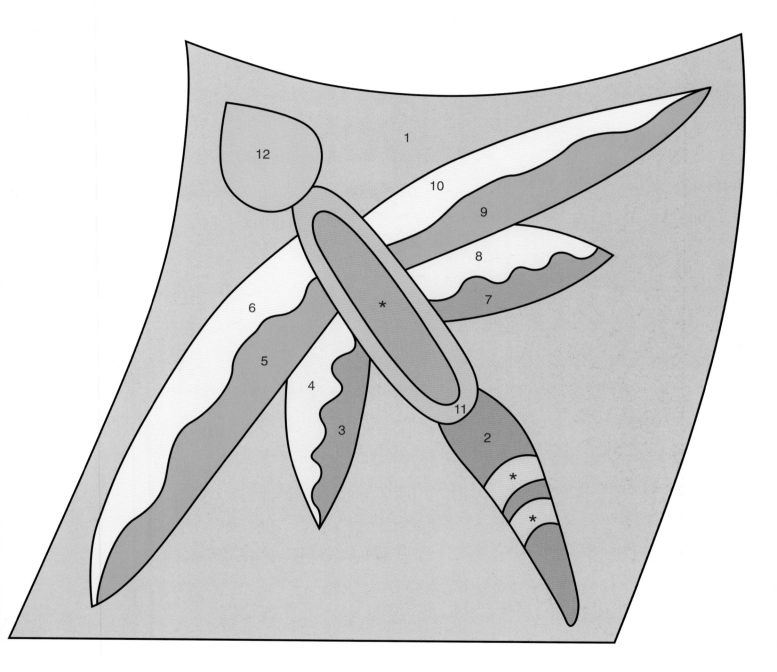

Full-size pattern

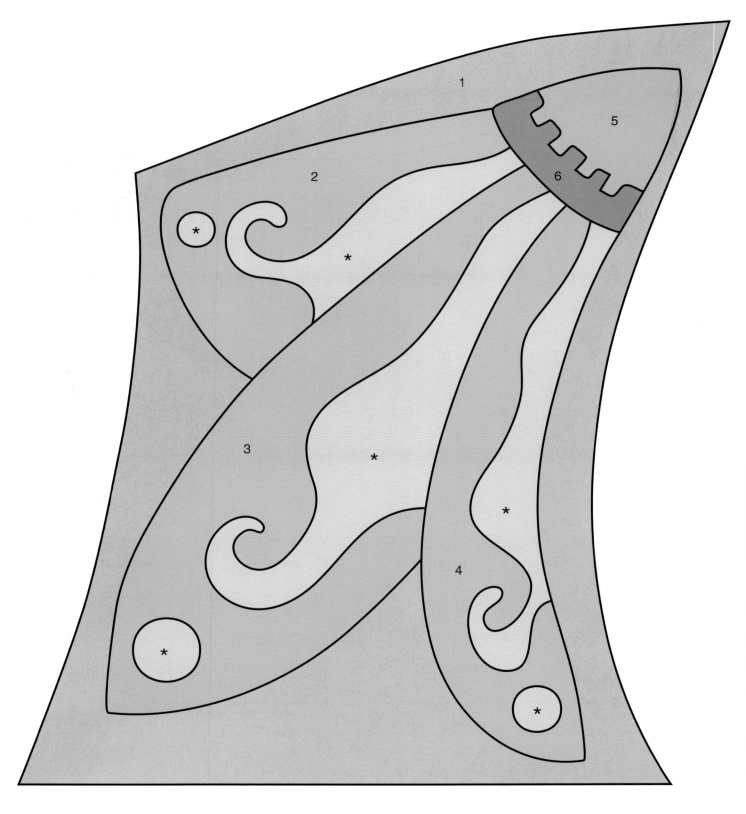

Appliqué a piece with an asterisk (*) to the underlying piece, then appliqué the unit to the background.

Full-size pattern

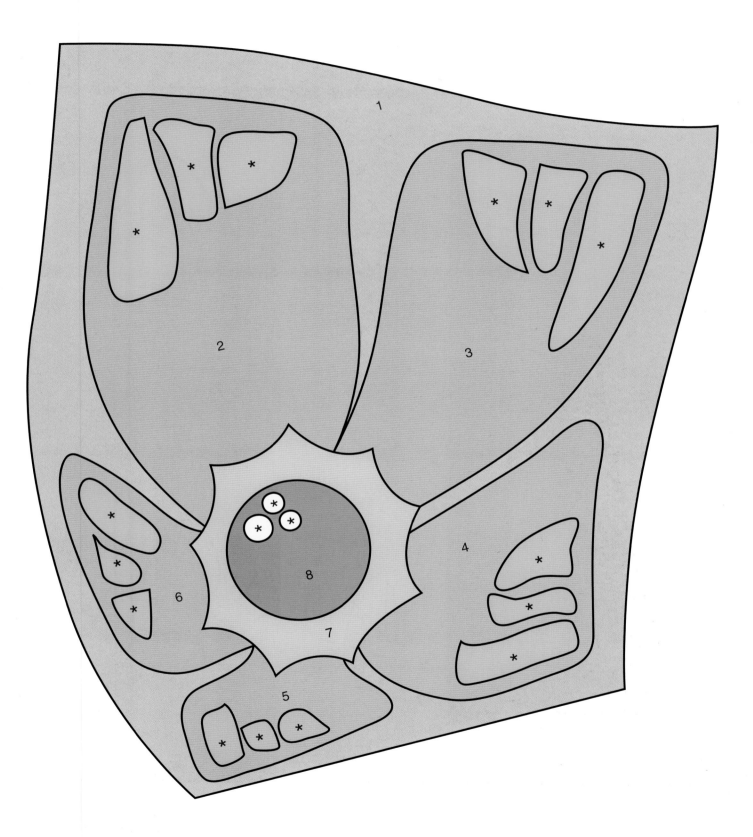

Full-size pattern

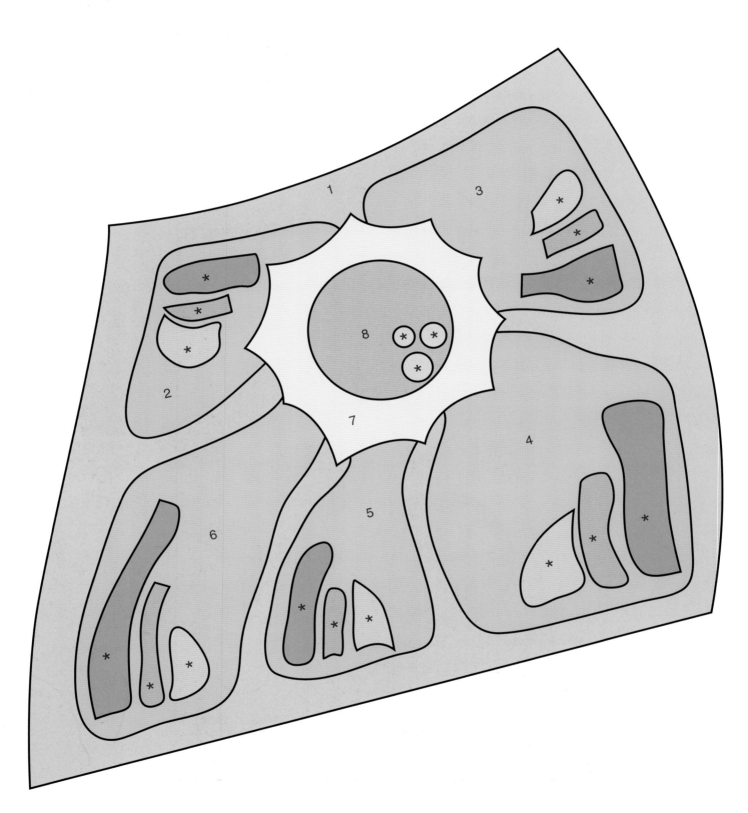

Appliqué a piece with an asterisk (*) to the underlying piece, then appliqué the unit to the background.

Full-size pattern

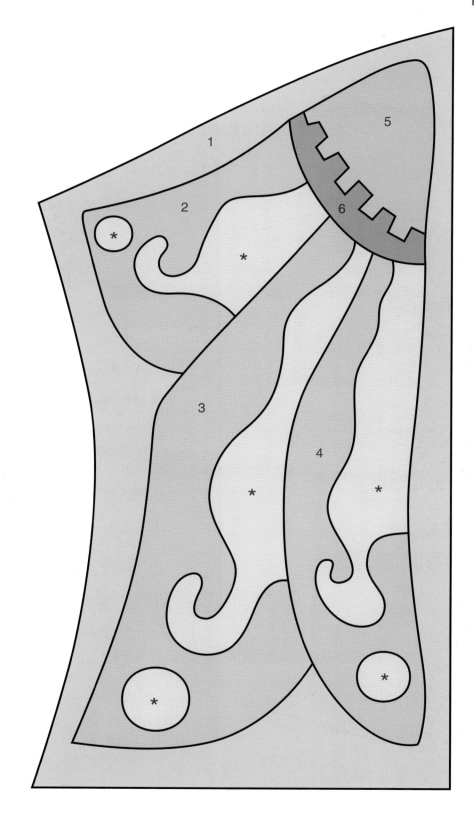

GALLERY

LOVE BLOOMS, 34½" x 42½"
A swirly heart is manifested in the center of a happy yellow bloom, filling my studio with thoughts of love and spring in February.

GREENHOUSE WINDOWS #1, 18½" x 20½"
This is the first in a series of quilts featuring "form fitting" flowers to free-form cut shapes. By fitting the flowers into the shapes, I gave myself permission to manipulate and warp forms. This added to a sense of whimsy. I have also begun to "frame" my quilts with off-set borders. I like this sense of off-balance and abstract perspective.

MINI SUN DAZEY #18, 9" x 10½"
This is a small version of one of my favorite characters, The Sun Dazey. I have been doodling this guy since high school, and he still makes me smile each and every time he waves hello from my studio shelf.

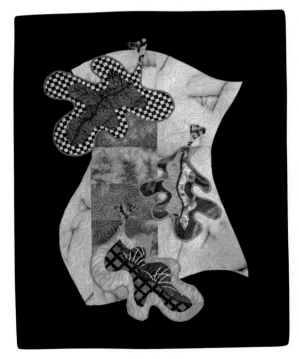

AUTUMN OAKS TRIO #3, 14" x 18"
Being a lifelong midwesterner, I know and enjoy a full four seasons annually. Autumn is by far my favorite. There is nothing more wonderful than a crisp autumn day with the leaves changing, the hot chocolate warming up on the stove, and a good football game on TV. Yes, I'm a sports fan too!

SUMMER BOUQUET, 16" x 10"
I love to make small garden quilts, especially on sunny days. This quilt features what I refer to as my "three toe roses" design. I cut these roses out by the dozens so I can just pick and choose when making my quilts – just like a florist.

AUTUMNAL JEWEL, 13" x 17"
A fantastic bead shop is only two blocks from my house. The call of the beads is quite strong. They are beginning to find homes in my quilts along with my wrist and ears.

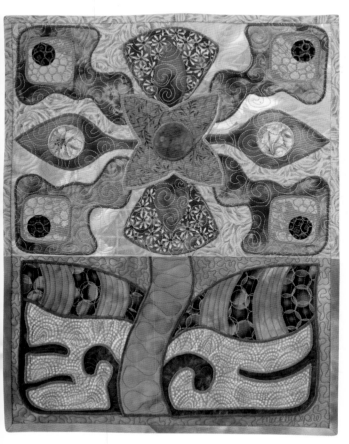

PETITE BLOCK GARDEN #5, 14" x 18"
This is a styled "blocky" flower that grew out of an artistic exercise of fitting a rounded object into a rectangular shape. I love this quilt – yellow flowers are my favorite.

SEEDLINGS, 53" x 43"
The joy of children – I like to think that even plants celebrate their seedlings!

RESOURCE GUIDE

The following manufacturers produce the products I use to make my quilts. While there are other products available, these are my favorites and work well in my projects. The Web sites will help you find their products at local quilt shops.

Décor-Bond®

Pellon®
www.pellonideas.com

Fabric

Bali Fabrics Inc.
www.balifab.com

Benartex, Inc.
www.benartex.com

Moda United Notions
www.unitednotions.com

Northcott Fabrics
www.northcott.net

Batting
Hobbs Bonded Fibers
www.hobbsbondedfibers.com

Sewing Machine

Bernina® of America, Inc.
www.berninausa.com

Thread

Superior Threads
www.superiorthreads.com

YLI® Bobbin & Lingerie Thread
www.ylicorp.com

WATER DROPLETS, 11" x 18"
This winter has brought a lot of rain and very little snow. A rainy January followed by a mild February, and possibly balmy March, will jumpstart my gardens. While I miss the snow terribly, maybe it isn't so bad.

MEET THE AUTHOR

And in the end it's not the years in your life that count. It's the life in your years.
— Abraham Lincoln

Sewing since early childhood, Mickey Depre began her quiltmaking journey in the late 1980s as an outlet for her creative spirit. After making a few traditional quilts, all was put aside with the arrival of her twins in 1990. She found her way back to quilting in 1997, when school sessions brought free time back into her life. Mickey says she will never leave quilting again.

Textiles have always fascinated Mickey, from vintage to current. Sewing in general – mending to garment making – was never a chore. However, when pushed beyond traditional quiltmaking, she found that the road less traveled was greatly inviting.

Her quilts have been described as whirlwinds of color, with oranges residing next to purples of all shades in harmony. Dots, swirls, and stripes intermingle with florals and prints in an outlandish, yet exciting visual parade. Mickey's work reflects how she sees the world and how she wants the world to see her.

Mickey's quilts mix traditional techniques with bold, innovative machine appliqué and threadwork. Fabric choices include her own hand dyes with commercial cottons for a special spark of color and depth. Pieces are heavily machine quilted while guided by hand. The images are meant to spark thought and a smile because she believes humor is a great gift to share.

Mickey can be contacted at www.mdquilts.com.

Other AQS Books

This is only a small selection of the books available from the American Quilter's Society. AQS books are known worldwide for timely topics, clear writing, beautiful color photos, and accurate illustrations and patterns. The following books are available from your local bookseller, quilt shop, or public library.

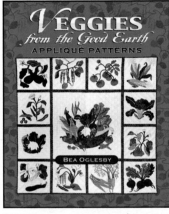

#7017   us$21.95

#6674   us$19.95

#7012   us$19.95

#6903   us$19.95

#6905   us$24.95

#6896   us$22.95

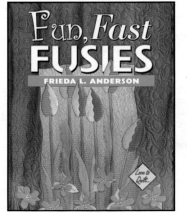

#6801   us$19.95

#6897   us$22.95

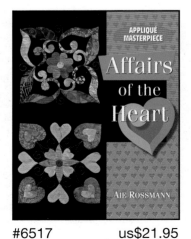

#6517   us$21.95

LOOK for these books nationally. **CALL 1-800-626-5420**
or **VISIT** our Web site at **www.AmericanQuilter.com**